APERTURE

A P E R T U R E

A N N A L E A H Y

Published in the United Kingdom in 2017
by Shearsman Books Ltd
50 Westons Hill Drive
Bristol BS16 7DF

Shearsman Books Ltd Registered Office
30–31 St. James Place, Mangotsfield. Bristol BS16 9JB
(this address is not for correspondence)

ISBN: 9781848615168

Book Design: Claudine Jaenichen
Cover Art: Lia Halloran
Typefaces: Univers by Adrian Frutiger and Utopia
by Robert Slimbach

Table of Contents

Flirting with Fugue

And then to play. The play's the thing. Play's the thing.
All virtue in 'as if.' —Robert Frost

If myth were a kiss,

    I'd pucker for the script.

If dreams were a dance,

    I'd skip-trip the overture

and look for the marquee.

    If life were a game of tag,

you'd be *it*, and I'd run

    from comedy to tragedy,

bend and come back again.

    If all politics were local,

you'd choose and be chosen

    our tart memento mori.

If virtue weren't the only thing,

    we'd play with our dowry.

The Absent Mothers
of *The Wizard of Oz*
Speak Out

Mrs. Marvel's Radio Interview

Where is your son now?

I imagine he's camped out on some country road. Selling
potions, promises, that sort of thing. He tried to get me
to believe all manner of hope. I wasn't buying it.

He disappeared long ago. That's what he wanted. Isn't that
what anyone wants—to leave someone behind?

*What have you been doing since your son struck out on
his own?*

Stewing. He'd be surprised to hear that, I bet. He'd be
surprised to know I give him a second thought. He left.
I'm what's left.

But he's probably made a name for himself, don't you
think?

*It sounds as if you want to believe that he's done something
worthwhile with his life.*

I'm willing to hope now. Convince me.

Mrs. Witch's Letter to Her Widowed Sister, regarding their daughters

The tongue illuminates consequences:
    my words go and others' come back.
One thought leads to another and to sentences
    we must utter, mawing the syllables
to get them swaggering back and forth
    between our sizeable lives,
enchanted by the spell we cast
    with our sinny-shiny syntax,
because just when we hear our own voices—
    sometimes sibilant, often labial, unvoiced,
occasionally, wonderfully guttural—
    we find that we are listening, too, off stage.
Indeed, we are as interested in each other
    as we are in ourselves.

Mrs. Tinman's Statement to the Press

He was always the sort of child who played
in the rain. The world leaked in, as I'd feared.
It became worse when his dad disappeared.
My son spent his time in the woods. I made

a promise not to follow him as long
as he carried his axe, though he'd never
use it. I wanted him to be clever,
not kind. To stay safe—was it so wrong

of me to want our family to mend here?
Of course, he didn't blame me—who could?
Still, he might have stayed, maybe done some good
if only I had let him be more tender.

If he does not return, I wish him well;
each of us has our own version to tell.

Mrs. Lion's Restroom Graffiti

The papers say my son is a coward.
  That's bullshit.
They say I must be a feminist.
  Was I supposed to raise a swine?
They edit out his father.
  Does he bear no role?

Mrs. Scarecrow's News Conference Statement

Small decisions always vexed him: corn or potatoes?
Right or left? Up or down? This or that little thing!
The less the decision mattered—so many don't much—
the more time he'd spend making it.

Right or left, up or down, this or that little thing:
everything kept him fix-focused until his head ached.
The more time he spent making one decision,
the harder the next one would be for him—for me—

our minds focused on fixing everything that ached.
It was difficult to watch. I tried to ignore it,
which was harder for me with each choice he faced.
The thing is, he knew most decisions didn't matter.

That's what made it difficult to watch so I tried to ignore
at least the small decisions that vexed him: corn or potatoes!
But nothing I did—or didn't do—seemed to matter to him.
Many decisions should have mattered much less.

Mrs. Gale's Posthumous Television Interview

How did you meet your own demise?

Childbirth was more than I could tolerate. I didn't last long
after that. Such things occurred regularly in those days.
My daughter spent three weeks in an incubator herself.

What did you expect to become of her?

I fully expected my husband to raise her, to find a new
wife, certainly, but to raise our child. His new wife had
other ideas, which was common at the time. I should
have known. My aunt and uncle took her in.

One time she saw her father at the racetrack, across a great
crowd, as if through a telescope. His newer daughter
wore an extravagant hat, glided up the stairs, her gloved
hand on the railing. The two girls looked a great deal
alike. They posed just the same way. They knew not to
speak to each other, even later.

Her father was a betting man.
I never understood odds.

What do you think has become of your daughter?

I hope she is traveling. That's something I was never able
to do. I see no good reason why she should ever return
home.

After Assassination

[…] I am perfectly sane, I do not desire to become insane.

—Mary Todd Lincoln,
August 8, 1875

I.

I remember the carriage ride, my hand in his hand for a change, my daily outing, usually solitary, happily imposed upon. We rode alone, unusual for him, always in dialogue. Washington unfurled around us on its spokes. I was easily lost, dizzied. I kept peeking around to orient myself instead of listening intently. I try to remember the plans we made that day. We would see California. I wanted to go all over Europe, to eat and shop. He wanted to see Jerusalem most of all. I try to remember our conversation, like running lines, what I said to him that he might have held in his thoughts, what his voice sounded like over the hooves clippity-clopping beneath us. I smoothed my dress with my hands, I remember.

II.

I smooth my hands over my dress still, a nervous
habit I took up in earnest the morning after, as if I
could be back in the carriage on that dreary-warm
day, before the theater, before the shot to the head,
before the doctor rushed in, before the body was
carried across the street, before our son arrived,
before the blood and the blood, which I could not
stop seeing, saying the word *blood* aloud in front of
everyone. My son held my wrists to stop me, but I
began again as soon as he let go: wailing and
smoothing, smoothing, smoothing my dress.
Repetition is the only thinking I can do. It seems
sudden to be in bed, my young boy at my feet, my
older son looking over, to be in Chicago, going on.

III.

I simply had migraine headaches, and migraine headaches were, as everyone who did not have them knew, imaginary.
—"In Bed," Joan Didion

Suddenly, we are back in Chicago. My son looks over everything. His oversight allows me to dwell on how I will live in the wake of my losses: my son, my husband, and now even my smarts, my wit, the exuberance that preceded our marriage, so much cropped out in a jump cut. I have only my petulant self of migraines and melancholy now and my trunks full of footstools, because I never found the just the right one, but couldn't keep myself from trying. My son is sending me off with my footstools and curtains. He's called for a carriage to take me to the train station in the morning. Unless the drugstore has laudanum—*shoulder pain,* I'll say. Or I'll go away, until I can be restored to reason.

IV.

History is hysterical: it is constituted only if we consider it, only if we look at it—and in order to look at it, we must be excluded from it.
—*Camera Lucida*, Roland Barthes

Reason is easily restored by a few weeks in the country and the realization that perhaps a woman who does not know what she is doing can have too many footstools and never enough friends, to whom I write in hopes they will remove me from the black-and-white circumstances in which I find myself. My son knows better. What is he after? I may amend my will. I take long walks, write letters, accept guests. My friends believe that I am well and make overtures on my behalf. Surely, I can manage my own affairs, they say. Surely, I am not a lunatic—not even my son would publicly declare otherwise. Where is the carriage to retrieve me, where that large hand in which to place mine? Where, sorrow?

Lizzie Siddal Looks
Back on Posing

Open not thy lips, thou foolish one,
Nor turn to me thy face:
The blasts of heaven shall strike me down
Ere I will give thee grace.

—from "Love and Hate," Elizabeth Siddal

Remembering *Ophelia* (1852)

I made a pretty painting,
secured a reputation
with *Ophelia*. The secret is
laudanum—the floaty-filmy feeling—
and the shiver-chill
when the fire went out
under the tub
and left my teeth to clatter;
that's what created my pallor,
gave the brush its worthy plot.
I held my quiet pose, always anxious
for verbal intercourse, though not
for the real thing.

On Hair

My red hair catches the eye.
I see it catch, like a spark, they say.
I see the artist think it worth preserving
rough cut with brushstroke or phrase.
Before this, I was raw stock,
didn't know I had anything to offer.
I made my way in millinery,
but it was brutal, that snip-and-stitch labor.
I have everything to offer.
I am eager to be sketched—
and to sketch, myself.
Before this, I didn't know that being inert,
edited for continuity,
makes its own glad-handed demands.

On Being Given a Name

Imagine a biography that includes not just a narrative
but also all the events that failed to foreshadow.
—*Ongoingness*, Sarah Maguso

It wasn't *Lizzie* that bothered me,
but the slashing off
the last letter of my last name.
And the worry
that I was not good enough
or not enough of or too much of
a good thing. The worry
that the light might leak
and ruin the master shot,
that he would turn his gaze
elsewhere, just when I'd grown
accustomed to his looking.

My Version (*The Lady of Shalott,* 1853)

Death by heartbreak:
on a stool at her loom

in a tower on an island,
out the window through the mirror,

turns her head, sees him ride
away, farther and farther.

The great unraveling:
from her hands all the threads,

in the mirror all the cracking,
on the floor, on the shelf,

the crucifix repeats itself.
My hand directs her stare;

she's a looker, eyes open.
What a delightful scene!

On Sketching *Pippa Passing the Loose Women* (1855)

I drew people well. I drew
people out of themselves, too.
These are unrelated talents,
but I was happy to have both abilities.

I portrayed good Pippa and the prostitutes
equally ably, virgin and harlot alike.
I captured their expressions:
mutual curiosity, earnest interest.

Even the geese stretch to see.
I rendered the human form well, too.
Render: to create a version,
to give something in return

like the women exchanging glances.
Rend: to slit, to split apart.

Laudanum

Tincture of opium: a suffusing
saturating permeating flood.

Over the counter
from the grocer, the barber, the baker.
A painkiller, a cordial
for irritable babies and bedwetting toddlers,
to alleviate cough, gout, menopause,
rheumatism, ulcers, cramps, bruises.
Nothing anyone suffered
could not be cured.

Hard to know whether sadness
is cause or effect, whether jealousy
is warranted or wanted, whether fatigue
comes or goes as a result,
whether weight is a figment,
whether subject matter, weightless.

I am drawn, so drawn.
I still hear that pun
as it weathers: the lasting for permanence,
the draining away under strain.

How much is enough?
A hundred drops in an evening will lead me
to the difference between
intransitive and transitive,
between *drop: slump, decline, fall, plunge*
and *drop: let go of, release.*

On Being *St. Catherine* (1857)

*I constitute myself in the process of "posing," I
instantaneously make another body for
myself, I transform myself into an image.*
—*Camera Lucida,* Roland Barthes

I imagined myself on the way
to have my body stretched over the wheel,
not later,
when the angels came
with lightning that sent spikes and splinters
into air. Clots everywhere. Tint-hints
of life lived, the filter removed.
I wouldn't have looked any happier then,
so it was a good thing
he painted the scene he painted:
my sulking self looking more pallid
than I knew, though if boredom
and the heft of such luxurious fabrics
could kill,
this painting might have done me in.
When I am beheaded, I thought,
milk will flow from my veins.
It was a relief not to be myself,
to see someone else's future
an alternate ending created
by switching the backdrop of existence.

Cast to Type (*How They Met Themselves*, 1851–1860)

I didn't need the inky doppelgangers
he made for us in Paris;
I hoped each of us was enough for the other.
Is it me fainting upon seeing myself,

or myself causing my other me to stumble?
This canvas was his longing
for reincarnation—that we had been reborn
as others or would be—not the life we lived.

This was my honeymoon swoon:
reading aloud, sketching each other's likenesses,
painting together, eating supper, and relief
when we returned home to England,

to our 180-degree existence, each of us
a raised surface in our marital engraving.

On Motherhood

I wouldn't have known much
what to do, what to do,
though I pretended
for a short while afterwards
with the empty cradle by the rocking chair,
where I rock-rock-rocked.
I left the loss for someone else to write—
and he did.

After that, I wanted it more
than ever, than anything,
all I could think about,
the only future I could imagine.
My desire became like that first posing:
a need to see
what I could make of myself,
to be stroked into being by flasback.

But I had long lost my ability
to sit, and my wanting came
with disbelief I couldn't suspend.

The Coroner's Verdict (1862)

After much testimony during the inquest
and numerous individuals claiming
no note, no self-injurious behavior,
no pessimism, no need to prevent proper burial,
the theatre's gone dark, stop
the rehearsal, there's no understudy, order the hearse,
my undoing was rendered accidental,
as death was common with laudanum
and various frailties I was thought to have—
after which I could be remembered
however one imagined.
Imagine me, please: dream me up!

Encore

Can you believe he exhumed me?
    Not me per se, but the poems
he'd buried with me when he thought
    sorrow could be as powerful as language,
only later to discover he was wrong,
    that sorrow was autumn in the heart,
and winter threatened to beget spring.

On Being *Beata Beatrix* (1870)

He captured more ecstasy than I had
mustered, frustrated by leaning forward
as if for a kiss, my lips parted, my eyes
closed, my mind lolling through the hours.
I wanted slumber but, later, couldn't
sleep, reeling through rushes, poppies and snow.

Three muses: song, occasion, memory—
voice itself, moment and motivation,
and recalling later. How convenient
that the field opened up before me—
how thankful I am that room was made.
Consequence is not only what is borne

but also what is borne out—and so,
we carry on, one and all, we carry on.

If I Had To Choose One Word

Cleave: itself and its opposite, all at once.

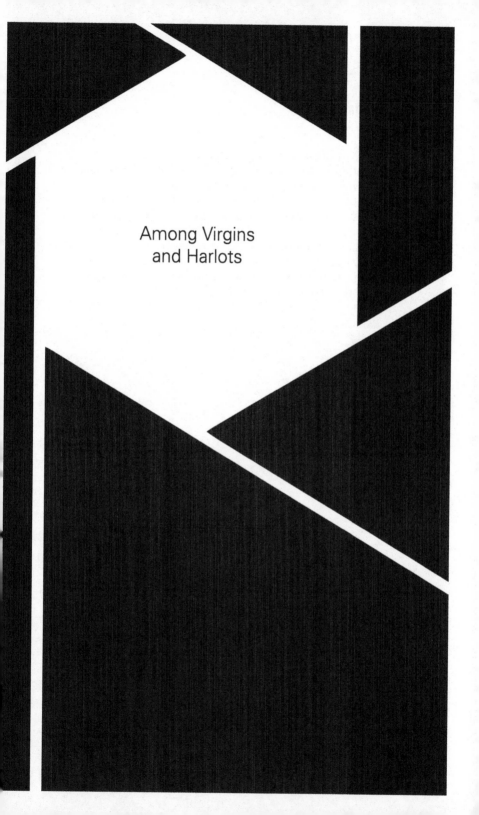

Among Virgins
and Harlots

Hagioscope

To see from the side chapel requires strabismus,
a condition cured by the snipping of eye muscles with scissors.
The world is what I see through this small hole
in a church wall, a squint, my body with eye to frame,
a kind of perpetual peeking, looking askance for the soul
as if sight did not depend on alignment. My eyes feel
the chalice's shape, color, the hands each
fitting exactly into the other, a blossom reaching,
rising, opening. My eyes taste the salty
wine, the lifeblood over the altar.

Conversing with Saint Catherine

Hers was the power of embers after fire
—"The Catherine Wheel," Nancy Kuhl

I.

May we say something instead of nothing;
May silence be more dangerous than speech;

May the most solemn vow be the voiced vow;
May we take breath enough, then part our lips;

May words come to us as they did to her
when she contradicted the philosophers,

when she said *no* to the emperor,
when the wheel broke apart and she said, *ha!*

Let our muscled tongues tickle each other's
ears. Let her repartee be our shrill guide;

Let her story say more about us than
it does about her; Let us invent it.

That would be good both going and coming back.
One could do worse than be a martyred saint.

II.

Talk, but not just chatter; Exchange,
something for something, given and taken;

When misused, tit for tat, one-upsmanship;
Done fluidly, a dance, arm in arm,

someone leading, someone following,
the curve of a firm back responding

to a rigid hand's insinuation
of virginity and harlotry;

A river, curving against its stiff banks,
changing direction, always supply coursing,

not again and again, but even yet.
What is the difference between banter

and narrative, if not the voices
and the (un)yielding bodies that craft them?

    III.

Girls in the mad rush before Advent plead:
    A husband, Saint Catherine,

    A good one, Saint Catherine,
    And soon, Saint Catherine.

What in the world were they thinking, praying
to a woman who refused marriage,

whose lesson was to make your own case,
whose feast day was dropped—lost, let loose—

because erasure is punishment
for making the whole thing up,

as if her imagined life was not worth living?
How do we say good-bye to someone

we thought we knew as well as anyone,
whose company we so thoroughly enjoyed?

The Musical Score: Saint Cecilia

Like birds, her fingertips light on the keys.
She's tuned and plays out of mind, out of sight
like crickets near dusk or owls dark at night.
She works up a sweat. She thinks she's a tree.
All limbs, Cecilia climbs into her tub:
the luminous score rises like wings,
the water boils like flocks of geese. It stings
blisters like feathers, scabs like leaves. She scrubs.

When this wet widow rises from her bath,
she bends with the breeze, then returns to her bench.
Her fingers are finches singing a riff
so she can't hear what's coming, nor whose wrath.
And when the axe hits her neck, her woody stench
fills the unsung world with organ music.

Rough Cut: Saint Margaret Mary

For I fear all things from my own weakness
—Saint Margaret Mary

with confusion and a pain comes
open chest its heart in-flaming
moments of waking are filled with

he the most perfect of lovers
bone body chained in want want not
what does he fear doubt coming in

early morning hours Margaret
nightmares revisit the fever
one woman expiates others

celebrate wild her feast death day
10:17 birth devotions
on the microwave clock *tick tock*

one minute not much like the next
for him film burned through flesh maybe
ashes reignite digging plans

maybe smother cocktail visions
a man with wet hands in his ribs
as convent embarks on career

save yourself glance mad away from
cardiovascular fountains
spew bright havoc on entrusted

love sex brilliance as if prayers
balding a smile rushed red ablaze
hope hangs itself silver medals

why not unbuild temples on strong
dashboard lies honestly spoken
as an open wound aflame

clings to blue eyes of have have not
yet he must look for what was is
not her but could be now later

in fire fear of too much household
or not enough inside moral
dilemmas mixed with messages

kiss the monstrance and bloody mend
delusional relics in words
this is my blood thorned pain on bone

what a clumsy dinner leads to
tasting familiar teeth and strange
breath on handed robes in knee fields

tangle figure twist arms as large
cry if you must choke if you can
supper last and feast me on you

Rehearsal: Saint Imelda

Too young, always too young,
they said, and so
Imelda placed petals
on her tongue
and let them dissolve
as practice for the rapture
for which she longed,
begging to anyone
who would listen.
She swallowed small stones
to feel them catch
near her heart
like a promise
and a promise broken.
Then, at Mass one day,
the wafer, like an angry
blue jay, flew at her.
Go ahead, if you must.
She died there,
with deliciousness melting
in her needy mouth,
just as she thought
anyone would
who really believed.

On Primping: Saint Mary Magdalene

That all is done, that I am free;
That you, through all eternity,
Have neither part nor lot in me.
—"Magdalen," Amy Levy

Seven devils and a striking face provide a young woman with certain opportunities. Modesty and moderation go—hand in hand—out the window. Everyone agreed her sins were many. Perhaps, she loved too much or too often, perhaps not a bit.

There are shrines, of sorts, to her on street corners: Tangles, Miss Snips, A Cut Above, Curl Up and Dye. Overcome, unbeguiled, she wept and had only her hair for a towel. Afterward, she massaged his feet with perfumed oils, perhaps seeing a divine big toe wriggle in reflex. What a surprise, an outrage even.

How difficult, then, it must have been to take his body down, anoint it again with oils and spices, and bury it. How tart on the heart's tongue.

For every bit of this, she was the first, without doubt, to see the body risen. Cut apart, fastened together—clipped. After that, no wonder she lived in a cave and trusted that breezes would feed her. Perhaps, she sucked on bruises like plums; perhaps, she doctored her kisses; perhaps, she tickled herself with her own locks and laughed—or sobbed—incessantly.

Aspect Ratio: Saint Agnes

[...] Even / the ravages of this old photograph / bloom
like water lilies across her thigh.
—"Bellocq's Ophelia," Natasha Trethewey

All the fathers she knew
were angry men. Her own father
slapped her sisters at the dinner table,
demanded manners, silence.
She put butter knives in her pockets.
By thirteen, to test herself,
she lured an angry
man with her pale lips around
a cigarette and her prayers.

Instruments of torture only challenged
her, their obviousness, their tragic
grips. She loved
the way they made her unable
to comfort anyone, the way they asked
her to do the very things
she wanted to do and avoid
that which she could not face,
the way they were not hands.

One suitor's father, terrified
with ache, stripped
her bare, led her through
the streets of Rome. *Look at this*
hypocrite, look at her wicked knees.
But her hair grew to remove
her shame, hide her cleavage, even
from her own view, to soothe her skin
because she stung with the thought
of being exposed.

In the streets, she called
out to married women, *be afraid and
forgive me.*
At the brothel, she called out
to men, *look at me, look at my body,
give me your eyes or I shall take them.*
And she struck any man blind
who looked at her. Then, she
cured any blind man
who wanted to look again.

When she was through, she wrote
letters like sickles
with short, sturdy handles and long,
curved blades. Angry
men are always subdued
by the confusion of fresh-cut grass,
green blades enchantingly askew.
She could reap what she slashed
or leave it to rot in the fields.

At thirteen, seduction is a kind
of miracle. Later, it looks
like witchcraft, the dimensions altered
by perspective, and the risk is
in the curing not the blinding.
Death came to her with unexpected
exhilaration, a sword through her throat
and the thrilled silence
that follows a slap to the face.
Onlookers wept, *she went more
cheerfully than a bride to her wedding.*

Outtakes: Saint Brigid

*I would like myself to be a rent payer to the Lord; that
I should suffer distress, that he would bestow a good
blessing on me.* —Saint Brigid

Sanctity: the shedding inside
of tissue after the masses

have developed secretly in sealed places
and must bleed, crying out a vow:

*Enough—a man
is no obligation,* and she digs

her index finger into her eye socket;
the moment an infant is named

by the breeze or a girl takes the veil
or a young woman sees the devil

at dinner; the point at which
a milkmaid's bathwater becomes

beer so the monks' thirst might be
quenched for eight days;

a presence at dusk, as when
wet robes hang on ropes of sun,

as when armies cannot see
each other for all their wanting

to kill and must return home with
their blind spots, as when the shadow

heals; the response, as when a namesake
ties a cloth to a branch over a stream,

dips her finger into a wet hollow the size
of the eyeball, and ingests

sanctioned remedies—*lupron, massage, raspberry
leaf, danazol, cauterization, aspirin, vitamin B$_6$, avoiding*

orgasm, eating oranges—to dispel
the pain that curses her into herself;

this girl has restored
the severed head, removed deadly

lesions, cured the requisite
leper, survived only on the milk

of a red-eared cow—
where does the blood go

if it is shed beneath the flesh,
somewhere in the soul,

and cannot surface,
will not conjure itself?

On Boredom: Saint Thérèse of Lisieux

It was then that the ecstasy and the dream began, in
which emotion was the matter of the universe, and
matter but an adventitious intrusion likely to hinder
you from spinning where you wanted to spin.
—*Tess of the d'Urbervilles,* Thomas Hardy

When her older sisters choose to flagellate
themselves and each other, she wishes her young
body could stand more than the inconvenience
of sleeping without a blanket, walking without light.
Her father's monkish silence leads to mistaken
Christmas gifts in her slippers. Her gratefulness
for his thinking she wanted
is a conversion from shyness to abandonment,
and a photograph of herself becomes evidence
of unembarrassed limitations to trust.
When her mother prospers with a lace business
of antimacassars and intricate table linens,
she cloisters herself, writes
the story of her soul at her abbess's request.
Where each day is demarcated by exactly
the same prayers and her abbess has wild
mood swings, she wishes she could, at least,
chasten herself with starvation awhile.
Where life consists of waiting for a fly
to light on her arm so that she can endure
the buzzing and then the tickling of flesh,
she might be ecstatic to find herself, one day,
coughing up blood for the next two years.
When death is a whispered chorus,
why not send showers of roses falling
with thorns spinning swiftly toward the earth?

Peep Show: Saint Agatha

There is no freedom in any circumstance where the
body is legislated, none at all. [...] We should have that
freedom, and that freedom should be sacrosanct.
—"The Alienable Rights of Women," Roxane Gay

The women of Aphrodesia crowd
around with their sweet scent of rising sweat.
There are deep moans from behind the scrim, shadows
commingling as one woman touches the back
of her hot neck with her slick fingers, whispers
yes, yes, Agatha. One moment
Agatha is surrounded by the bodies
of women, a dance of oscillating arms
and arching backs and pointed toes,
and the next minute her limbs are pulled
from their sockets and the rod says *now.*
And the next moment and the next.
The soles of her feet burn off,
she hears her own skin preach, smells
the flesh leaving. And the next consecrated moment
she holds her own breasts, warm from her chest,
heavy in her hands, the weight
of nipples and ducts, looks at their shape, hemoglobin
ringing through fingers,
her hands so full of herself,
chiming *this is all you have.*
And the next, a man's hands caress
each swollen areola. *You are whole, Agatha.*
She draws a small black hole, dark and expanding,
flooded with light that cannot escape.

Dissolve: Saint Margaret of Cortona

Each morning she places eight stones in each
shoe, slips feet into vamped prayer. In summer,
she wears a hairshirt, feels every stiffness
against her skin, on cue, all of it raw.

These are the ways she has come to know where
she ends and the world begins. *Where motive
dries, Margaret, and where it is still wet.*
Each evening, she holds hot coals to her

chest and thighs. Her flesh is a voice singing.
Listen. On Sundays, she places pebbles
in her bedeviled son's shoes and tells him
to run. Their bodies are offerings, penance

for their illegitimacy, their needs.
Your knight is slain, Margaret, forget him.
Your father will never forgive you.
Most days, she does not eat, does not sleep.

She accepts that in the space between
her body and what is not her body
lies mercy. *Touch a man with hot, ruddy hands.*
When she dies, her body does not rot,

hands, shoulders, ankles, lungs, incorrupt throat,
a montage of what she is and is not.
You are holy now, Margaret, and forever.
The backstoried stones have become her feet.

On Nervous Breakdowns:
Saint Dymphna

When wives die too young, husbands
buck up, grow beards, and make new love.
They sit down to eat,
and while cutting meat,
they pray for some sign from above.

Her father's long gaze in his grief
soon projects a fear in her chest
because she can see
the one she might be.
In mirrors, her image, when dressed,

looks like her mother. In her sleep,
she snores like the devil. Awake,
she crawls in a box
and alters her looks
as if she can make herself fake.

When Dymphna does chores, she dances
with forks, gives bowls a good toss.
Why must this girl weep
when she irons, creep
when she dusts, then mop up her loss?

To be famous, holy, and mad!
Are saints really artists of God
whose hands are the can-
vas reaching for plans
with brushes that strike them as odd?

She places slim fingers in ears.
She pokes at her eyes, up her nose.
She plugs herself up,
then runs to a hut
with a leash for the devil, a noose.

Her father can follow the coins
she pays on her way. When he nears,
   she hides in a book
   whose faith she mistook—
she is killed by the sword that she fears.

Dead, she forces the townsfolk in Gheel
to house the most loony, swoony
   of girls. They are her
   in disguise, with a whir
between hues and eyes like two spoons

reflecting what they must have thought
they wanted to be: a pun,
   safe flatware, a faint.
   Do girls learn to paint
to make a new face, to be shunned?

Every pigment leaves little wounds.
When Dymphna was young, did she think,
   yes, I'll be a martyr
   or just miss her mother?
This pushes us all to the brink.

Depth of Field: Saint Joan

And what was done within? Within the light
Through the rich gloom of pictured windows flowing,
Tinged with soft awfulness a stately sight—
—"Joan of Arc at Rheims," Felicia Hemans

within the light
her mother's voice on fingertips
she counts the takes
I love you Joan (I love you not)

the reddish light
still stained a saint one louder still
with words and twigs
a woman always forms her flame

scar scones in mouth
a mother's recipe for knives
in mother's lungs
think but do not say: *love me, hate*

the yellow dust
wears trousers swings her weapon crazed
to be a man
from whom women should rise away

inside the seethe
the armor white and outside clean
begins again
prayers will always cause some pain

the naïve green
to shift responsibility
for state or sex
some women will not dig their graves

lead outlines slice
figures released into church air
big feet, huge hands
rebirthed a soldier-daughter

who spurs her steed
its flanks in wound her own or his
arm handle blade
this body hates its very limbs

within blue cast
Joan dismantles her varied parts
she charms disguise
a daughter soon repeats herself

inside the night
she clubs women in their beds
fingers their lips
this soldier does a doubletake

the dark brown light
that cannot love itself but must
cloak the holy
under wishing mothers silent

picture windows
in which this woman reigns the scene
shrieking war cries
the color of her mother's voice

come closer I
will love you closer I will kill
the fire-light burns
beneath her fire must burn enclosed

Joan tongues old words
she steps inside her own stained glass
not sharp when whole
but story on the verge of split

(Under)(Over)Exposure: Saint Barbara

Place your hands between your thighs,
feel the blueberry bruises.
She is consumed with the axis of action,
that separation that makes the just-ahead real,
fascinated by the tangles in her hair
and her awkward young fingers.
Wipe yourself with whatever is available,
wash yourself with wet miracles.
She pulls out strands of her hair,
pinches each white root between
teeth, watches it fall from the tower's windows
like small brown birds unlearning to fly.
Breathe deeply to forget, breathe
deeply to remember.
Her priest, her physician, does not understand;
she vomits in the confessional
trying to tongue good words through her teeth
as if seduction weren't power too.
Write your story in a letter to a woman.
Seal it, send it, wait, silent, for a reply.
Her father disapproves of the third window,
the extra light, the extra access. All the while,
she combs her lengthening hair,
hears her lover beckon, lets down
her hair, taking him fully
into her tower, into her mouth
until he writhes away in a dream.
She must find her own way back.
A whip is a dead snake, your voice cracks.
Her father thinks she has been consumed
by the holy spirit, that her kneeling is joy.
She endures what the village has to offer,
her arms spread to bending tree limbs.
A hammer's face is like a finger, the same shape,
the same source, and at the other end
a claw.
She runs, hides in a cave, speaks with thunder.
Curse the evil shepherd who does not hide you.

His flock will be locusts and he, stone.
Her father drags her by her hair
up a mountain, wind snapping
like children playing with firecrackers.
Your father must die.
Lightning will strike cancer into his bones,
and he will become ash.
With the knife he uses for sheep slaughter,
he slices her neck and holds her head up
by its matted, mad hair, a trophy.
Swing in the breeze, woman. Leak.

Continuity: Saint Ann

The sainthood of a woman demands the belief that irony is a powerful force in the universe, a right and left hand, the obstacle and the means. Take Saint Ann, who was grandfathered into the canon, who did not earn her halo the hard way. A retroactive saint. Rider of her daughter's coattails. By the time the Church wanted to canonize her, no one remembered her name. The Old Testament Hannah—Ann—was good enough: another advocate of late-in-life copulation. Lives spliced.

The Immaculate Conception, despite some confusion, is Ann's uterus uncarnal for the occasion, able to endure sex without, just that once, original sin staining the mollycoddled result. No wonder her daughter's whole body deserved Heaven. Mary, full of grace, full of Ann which means grace, must have been an easy child to raise. But a more difficult wife.

Centuries later, Ann sent Martin Luther an umbrella in a thunderstorm so that he would enter the priesthood. Susceptible to symbols. Then, he shut her up in a whoosh, claimed she was un-historical. But in medieval times, people couldn't get enough of her, venerating with fervor. Pope Urban VI let her cozy up church to state, made her feast obligatory in England when Richard II married her namesake of Bohemia. Even now, her valuable head is on display in Lyons and Chartres—for she vacationed there with the young Jesus—and also on display in Bologna, in Sicily, in Germany. She lost her head everywhere.

Here's to Ann, patron saint of miners, black lung disease, canaries, claustrophobia, minerals. Here's to hindsight. And gratitude for teaching the mother of God to read.

Shooting Ratio

It is no accident that the photographer becomes a
photographer any more than the lion tamer becomes
a lion tamer. —Dorothea Lange

Sainthood: the serendipity
of virgins and whores, one and all,
all of us among them,

one tracking mistake after another,
the mistranslation, the slip of our tongues
into the wrong ears, no accident,

the ears surprised—no surprise, all surprise—
by the difference between a life lived
and what's remembered on the mind's screen.

Take Agnes, the sound of her name
and, hence, the iconography:
the lamb—the Latin *agnus*—in her arms.

Or Agatha, her breasts shaped
like bells: the patron of bell ringers.
Or Thérèse, whose life was so boring

that she protects those who wish
no excitement: patron of pilots.
Bibiana is the Spanish sound

of Latin consonants,
full of life or full of drink,
who's to say?

Had she been drunk,
would that explain the scourging
she ably took?

Had she been exuberant,
why would she not curse
and swear: talk back!

Awash

As a charm against the terror of the unseen I have, for many years now, always entered the water silently repeating this command: Trust the water.

— Eula Biss, "No-Man's-Land"

Learning to Swim

Water, water, everywhere, and not a drop to drink.
—my grandmother

Who are we to be rudderless
   without fins, held
      in arms, in glances, in poses?

My father could not swim; my mother could.
   Sometimes, it's best to close one's eyes,
      become whole with fingers synced;

the power hardly jars us.
   Breath glides like ink.
      Salt crystals emerge as our hair dries.

Between Scylla and Charybdis

A woman, like any good sailor, knows
   the story of the sea's clashing rocks.
      She sends a white bird through

and times the safe opening that follows—
   the hands between clap—
      the oars row, the bow gasps forward,

the rocks just clip the stern.
   She notices then the remnants
      of crushed ships. Planks, tailfeathers.

Once passed, in the past, the threat becomes stationary
   as if a single success nullifies future risk
      and the houselights come on.

Ink

Felicia Hemans, 1818

She waves to the captain,
  her breasts let down.
    She imagines her infant

a harp held to her cleavage
  before she jumps off a cliff,
    falls with her face to the sky,

hands catching sun like salt through fingers.
  She thinks ink is the color of the darkening ocean,
    some poems drown some women,

children's voices break with frothy curls.
  His sailing's no loss. In this composition,
    she sips until her lips part.

Evidence of Grace

Saint Eulalia, circa 304 A.D.

If a girl believes
    the ocean is evidence of grace,
        how can she swallow

her soliloquy? When a girl speaks out
    of turn, she isn't well tolerated,
        must set her hair on fire:

smoke signals like prayers. Smothered, she gives up.
    From her open mouth, flies a single bird.
        Her body goes dark, becomes ash.

Snow settles to cool
    her remains. If love were deserved, girls would be
        always half full.

Lady of the Lighthouse

Ida Lewis, over a fifty-year career

Lady of the lighthouse, lady as the lookout: mistaken
    sailors waiting, wet-weighted.
        One, two: father strokes out.

Three, four: a good night's catch.
    Five, six: save another batch.
        Year after year, the darkness

brings men to her. She beaches men, pulls them
    out of the breakers, out by their breeches.
        Seven, eight: drowsy and doused.

Nine, ten: the dowry's spent.
    Eleven, twelve: hoist men drenched.
        Night after night, she lights the waves,

wastes her breath on the ancient sea,
    waits for mariners in the wake.
        The lantern dissolves. She sleeps at dawn.

Wife of a Whaler

Mary Patten, 1856

Wife of a whaler, wife
   on a war ship, consort on a clipper,
     captive below deck, motion sick,

morning sick. The winds pick up,
   the ship drifts south, the ice glosses over.
     When her captain falls ill,

fails her, and the crew is at a loss,
   she navigates the Cape, is capable
     of anything. Nothing less will do.

She reads stars like stitches
   in the capacious night; she follows
     the seam to the edge of cloth.

If Wishes Were Waves

The Lusitania, 1915

A woman pans for death: the horizon
    moves, heads pendulate, slow bobbins
        unwind their thread, skin fails, teeth chatter,

crack, black skirts seep away.
    A woman is numb before she dies.
    Pulled from the sea or washed up,

the bodies are laid out
    exposed on the cobblestone and photographed.
    No one can tell who belongs to whom,

one body and then the next: depth of field.
    Does a woman with needle and thread
        prick a stitch into each eyelid to seal the sinking?

In Love and War

All photographs are memento mori. *To take a photograph is to participate in another person's (or thing's) mortality, vulnerability, mutability. Precisely by slicing out this moment and freezing it, all photographs testify to time's relentless melt.*
—On Photography, Susan Sontag

A good pilot in battle over water
    keeps flightplans bound in lead covers—
      if I have to ditch my bird, my heart,

my codes will sink quickly out of reach.
    Imagine the ocean's floor full of love's litter:
      the lead-laced intentions, someone's

Spitfire full of holes. Who am I to think
    I will make the return trip, wingtip
      to wingtip with another lucky crew,

my gunners spreading fire in our track,
    my photographers collecting images
      I have no time to see for myself?

If I dare to look back, I will see I made mistakes,
    miscalculated my attitude by a few degrees,
      nagged his shore too soon after dusk.

Who's to say which sordid sortie will do me in,
    leave me thirsty in some unromantic life raft,
      the lusty propeller noise distancing itself?

The Physics of Denouement

Marie Curie, 1910

Speed and duration cause mood swings.
   Gravity and pressure, heartbreak.
   Dragged by the air,

caught up and then pulled away
   in repeated effort and failure,
    water seems blue when it has depth.

Like Fruit

Hurricane, 1900

In Galveston, the gulf rises
   to the treetops, rises above rooftops.
     The strip of land and the sea

indistinguishable. When the water recedes,
   long-haired women
     dangle from limbs.

Locals harvest strands of pearls
   like fruit and leave
     the looted beauties sleeping.

The Waves

Virginia Woolf, 1931

She cannot pay attention
    to much but the water's luscious
      slapping, the chaos

and the rhythm emerging only to fail,
    like lead geese falling back, replaced,
      or like a crowd clapping, hands

in and out of sync. She tries to adjust to the sound
    of *inseparable* as if hearing is enough
      to make sense of herself.

My Mother's Mermaid

Esther Williams, circa 1946

She is sequined and slicked down
   with emeralds in her hair, mouth
      puckered and wordless red.

A wave of her hand, music strikes up.
   A chorus line loops below, the body in water
      with so many legs spreading:

she dives, sparkles, swims like virtue,
   crotches like roofbeams above.
      The water rushes her teeth.

She rises like a voice from a clear throat
   as if passion were technicolor myth,
      as if the sea were the means

for the story I tell
   instead of the story itself,
      the thing that tells me.

Coda

Trajectory

After Katherine Johnson, mathematician

*When you can feel that close to something you're used to
seeing at that great distance, well, it changes a person.*
—Sally Ride, astronaut

Star sailor, history's tailor, spacefarer,
    how far she needled your path through space,

past blue halo, our circle of vapor,
    past the vast figure-eight of plasma swathes,

how near to infinity and back.
    That happy past has gone by, is bygone,

and then it came slapping back again,
    booming on boosters, rolling upside down,

catching its breath as if overcoming
    dynamic forces requires only great

inspiration. Will posterity shear
    gravity along the seam, trail a wake,

wake us? She stitched astronauts' trajectory,
    the warp and weft of history.

The Habits of Light

After Henrietta Leavitt, astronomer

The difference between luminosity and brightness
is the difference between being

and being perceived, between the energy emitted
and the apparent magnitude. O, to be

significant! To have some scope and scale!
Size and heat. Why not make that obvious,

ostensible, stretch it out for all the world to see?
Distance makes a world of difference.

The universe is made of distance and of dust.
More dust than star out there,

more crimson than cobalt from here, looking,
our eyes telling the truth slant

through the almost-nothing
of the universe's finely grained mattering.

Notes

Flirting with Fugue
The epigraph is from Robert Frost's "Introduction to Robinson's *King Jasper,*" available in *Robert Frost: Poetry & Prose* (Holt, Rinehart and Winston, 1972).

The Absent Mothers of *The Wizard of Oz* Speak Out
The Wizard of Oz is a book by L. Frank Baum, published in 1900. The film adaptation was released by MGM in 1939. Several other literary and cinematic versions have followed.

After Assassination
The section's epigraph is excerpted from a letter by Mark Todd Lincoln as quoted in Jason Emerson's *The Madness of Mary Lincoln* (Southern Illinois UP, 2007). The epigraph for Section III is from Joan Didion's "In Bed" in *The White Album*, which is collected in *We Tell Ourselves Stories in Order to Live* (Knopf, 2006). The epigraph for Section IV is from Roland Barthes' *Camera Lucida* (Farrar, Strauss and Giroux, 1981).

Lizzie Siddal Looks Back on Posing
Elizabeth Siddal (1829-1862) was an artist's model, a painter, and a poet associated with the Pre-Raphaelites. The opening epigraph is from Siddal's "Love and Hate," which appears in *Victorian Poetry and Poetic Theory* (Broadview, 1999). The epigraph for "On Being Given a Name" is from Sarah Manguso's *Ongoingness: The End of a Diary* (Graywolf, 2015). The epigraph for "On Being *St. Catherine* (1857)" is from Roland Barthes' *Camera Lucida* (Farrar, Strauss and Giroux, 1981). The epigraph for "On Motherhood" is from Lia Purpura's essay "On Aesthetics" in *On Looking* (Sarabande Books, 2006).

Among Virgins and Harlots
The epigraph for "Conversing with Saint Catherine" is from Nancy's Kuhl's poem "The Catherine Wheel," which is included in *The Wife of the Left Hand* (Shearsman, 2007); the final two lines of Section I echo Robert Frost's "Birches," which is widely available in print and online. The epigraph for "On Primping" is from Amy Levy's poem "Magdalen," which is included in *The Complete Novels and Selected Writings* (UP of Florida, 1993). The epigraph for "Aspect Ratio" is from Natasha Trethewey's poem "Bellocq's Ophelia" in the book by the same title (Graywolf, 2002). The epigraph for "On Bordeom" is from Thomas Hardy's novel *Tess of the d'Urbervilles*, which is widely available. The epigraph

for "Peep Show" is from Roxane Gay's "The Alienable Rights of Women" in *The Bad Feminist* (Harper Perennial, 2014). The epigraph for "Depth of Field" is from Felicia Hemans's poem "Joan of Arc at Rheims," which is included in *Records of Women with Other Poems* (UP of Kentucky, 1999). The epigraph by Dorothea Lange for "Shooting Ratio" appears in "A Brief Anthology of Quotations" in Susan Sontag's *On Photography* (Farrar, Strauss and Giroux, 1977). Other epigraphs in this section are adapted from *Prayers of the Saints* (HarperOne, 1996).

Awash

The epigraph for this section is excerpted from Eula Biss's essay "No-Man's-Land," which appeared in *The Believer* in 2008. My grandmother's words that serve as the epigraph for "Learning to Swim" are a colloquial adaptation of Samuel Taylor Coleridge's poem "Rime of the Ancient Mariner," which is widely available. The epigraph for "In Love and War" is from Susan Sontag's "In Plato's Cave," which opens her book *On Photography* (Farrar, Straus and Giroux, 1977).

Coda

The epigraph for "Trajectory" is from an interview with space shuttle astronaut Sally Ride, the first American woman in space, by Margaret McMullan for *Glamour*. In 1938, Katherine Johnson became one of the first three African-Americans at West Virginia University. She later worked for NASA, where, among other contributions, she calculated the trajectories for the first American manned space mission and for the Apollo 11 mission to land on the Moon. Henrietta Leavitt, as a human computer in Edward Pickering's so-called harem at the Harvard College Observatory, discovered the relationship between luminosity and the regular period of brightness in variable stars, a discovery that led Edwin Hubble to determine that the universe was expanding; Hubble acknowledged Leavitt's equal role when he accepted the Nobel Prize for his discovery.

Acknowledgments

I am grateful to the editors who published the following poems, sometimes in different versions.

The Account: "On Being *Beata Beatrix* (1870)"

Barn Owl Review: "On Nervous Breakdowns: Saint Dymphna"

Comstock Review: "The Habits of Light"

Crab Orchard Review: "After Assassination"

dirtcakes: "My Mother's Mermaid" and excerpts of "The Absent Mothers of *The Wizard of Oz* Speak Out"

Image: "The Musical Score: Saint Cecilia" (as "Saint Cecilia") and "Shooting Ratio" (as "Saint Bibiana")

Jeopardy: "On Primping: Saint Mary Magdalene" (as "Saint Mary Magdalene")

Margie: "Like Fruit" (as "Hurricane, 1900")

Mayday: "On Laudanum," "On Being St. Catherine (1857)," and "Remembering Ophelia (1852)"

Nimrod: "Awash" (excerpts published as a series)

Oberon: "Conversing with Saint Catherine"

Queen Mob's Teahouse: "Trajectory" (as "What I Want to Be When I Grow Up")

ROAR: "Flirting with Fugue"

Sou'wester: "Rehearsal: Saint Imelda" (as "Saint Imelda")

The section "Lizzie Siddal Looks Back on Posing" appeared as the chapbook *Sharp Miracles,* published by Blue Lyra Press in 2016.

"Mrs. Witch's Letter to Her Widowed Sister" appeared as "Incantation" in the chapbook *Sharp Miracles* and in the *Her Mark Calendar 2010,* published by Woman Made Gallery in Chicago.

"On Sketching *Pippa Passes the Loose Women* (1855)" appears in *A Face to Meet the Faces: An Anthology of Contemporary Persona Poetry* from the University of Akron Press in 2012.

"On Boredom: Saint Thérèse" (as "Saint Thérèse: Patron Saint of Pilots") and "In Love and War" (as "Warbird") appear in the chapbook *Turns about a Point,* which was published by Finishing Line Press in 2006.

Some poems in the section "Among Virgins and Harlots" appear in the chapbook *Hagioscope,* which won the Sow's Ear Poetry Prize in 2000.

Thanks to Tony Frazer and Shearsman Books for sharing this collection with the world and also to Claudine Jaenichen of Jaenichen Design for her expertise and care. Thanks to Lia Halloran for use of her artwork, *Barred Spiral (after Henrietta Leavitt).*

Thanks to Dorland Mountain Arts Colony and Ragdale, where some of these poems were drafted or revised, and to the American Library in Paris, where the final proofreading was completed.

I am grateful to Nancy Kuhl, Margaret Cullen, Brigid Leahy, and especially Douglas R. Dechow, all of whom helped me to shape this collection in one way or another.